PLATONISM AND THE
SPIRITUAL LIFE

PLATONISM AND THE SPIRITUAL LIFE

BY

GEORGE SANTAYANA

LONDON

CONSTABLE AND CO. LTD.

1927

First Published 1927
Reprinted   1927

PRINTED IN GREAT BRITAIN.
CHISWICK PRESS: CHARLES WHITTINGHAM AND GRIGGS (PRINTERS), LTD.
TOOKS COURT, CHANCERY LANE, LONDON.

PLATONISM
AND THE SPIRITUAL LIFE

I

INTELLECTUAL anarchy is full of lights; its
blindness is made up of dazzling survivals,
revivals, and fresh beginnings. Were it not
for these remnants or seeds of order, chaos
itself could not exist; it would be nothing.
Without demanding from the men of to-day
anything final or solid we may be grateful to
them for those glimpses of great things past
and of great things possible, which flash
through their labouring minds. One of these
great things past is Platonism, and one of the
great things always possible is spiritual life.
There is, or there seems to be, a certain affinity
between these two, as if deep called unto deep.
Yet I am not sure that everything in Platonism,
or even its first principles, can be called
spiritual; nor is it easy to discern what the
essence of spirituality may be, entangled as its
manifestations have always been with all sorts
of accidental traditions and prejudices.

In this perplexity I find a list of points

common to Platonism and to "spiritual religion" drawn up by the competent hand of the Dean of St. Paul's.[1] These points are "a firm belief in absolute and eternal values as the most real things in the universe—a confidence that these values are knowable by man—a belief that they can nevertheless be known only by whole-hearted consecration of the intellect, will, and affections to the great quest —an entirely open mind towards the discoveries of science—a reverent and receptive attitude to the beauty, sublimity, and wisdom of the creation, as a revelation of the mind and character of the Creator—a complete indifference to the current valuations of the worldling." This faith "is distinguished, among other things, by its deep love of this good and beautiful world, combined with a steady rejection of that same world whenever it threatens to conceal, instead of revealing, the unseen and eternal world behind. The Platonist loves . . . Nature, because in Nature he perceives Spirit creating after its own likeness. As soon as the seen and the unseen worlds fall apart and lose connection with each other, both are dead." " Values are

[1] Cf. *The Platonic Tradition in English Religious Thought*, the Hulsean Lectures at Cambridge, 1925-6, by William Ralph Inge, Dean of St. Paul's, etc., Longmans, Green and Co., London, 1926. All the phrases quoted are drawn from this book.

for the Platonist not only ideals but creative powers."

This, of course, is the language of a modern. Dean Inge is not quoting Plato or Plotinus, but expressing what he believes to be substantially their view in words natural to a man of his own country and religion. We must, therefore, puzzle a little and hazard a guess before we can recall the Platonic tenets to which some of these phrases may refer. The term " value " in particular is subjective, imageless, and in a manner evasive. It may be taken as a neutral term fairly representing the common quality of what Plato called the good and the beautiful, before these were hypostatized; but then to hypostatize not only such values, but all natural types and logical concepts, was the very soul of Platonism; and when the good and the beautiful have been hypostatized and have become God or the One, the Ideas, the Demiurgus, or the Soul of the World, they are no longer values, but independent beings, existing long before the need or the admiration of mortals could attribute any value to them. Value is something relative, a dignity which anything may acquire in view of the benefit or satisfaction which it brings to some living being. If God or the Ideas were mere values, as are pleasure or health, they would be unsubstantial, and only a desired or achieved perfection in something else. They might, indeed, have value in their own eyes, but only if they were alive. A man, or a god, cannot prize his existence before he exists. An automatic harmony must be established in his life before he can distinguish its direction, suffer at its diminution, or conceive and desire its greater perfection. This harmony itself is a good only because the spirit which it creates so regards it.

II

IF I were a theologian, or even a bishop, I
might be innocently led to ask Dean Inge what
he means by a value. Is it anything that anybody values, or only that which some other
person thinks we ought to value? Is it the
fact that some satisfying aspect is found in
things, or rather a magic necessity providing
that such an aspect shall be found there? Or,
as we gather from other Cambridge philosophers,[1] is this necessity not magical but natural
and omnipresent in things, so that whenever
a wave rises and bursts into foam, or a snow-
flake takes shape in the air, or any other form
trembles for a moment in the flux of existence,
the realization of this visiting essence is intrinsically a value, whether it be watched and
prized by any spirit or not? Or on the contrary are values existing supernatural beings,
by their influence compelling or inclining
nature often to reproduce these satisfactory
aspects? And I might even like to ask, going
a little deeper, whether such supernatural
beings, granting that they exist, work in
nature towards the production of values of any

[1] For instance, in Whitehead's *Science in the Modern
World*.

and every sort—as the law of the survival of the fittest might work to produce harmony between each sort of animal and its habitat, but to make their forms and their pleasures more and more diverse—or whether these supernatural beings are biassed in favour of certain natural forms and certain values to the exclusion of others; and finally, whether it is this congenital bias in supernatural powers that we should understand by the eternal reality of values.

In the modern notion—a very hazy one—that values themselves might be forces there is a contradiction, or at least an ellipsis. In any single instance, indeed, a mind disinclined to look for the causes or origins of things may find in an actual value a final and satisfying fact. Felt values reconcile the animal and moral side of our nature to their own contingency: if anything is well, we neglect to ask why it happens. The inner connivance and peace of our will explain it sufficiently. But when values are supposed to sustain themselves in being through a long tangle of circumstances, and to reassert themselves intermittently by their own strength, we are not merely content not to inquire why they arise, but we profess to explain their occasions and causes by their future presence: a position not only impossible to defend, but impossible to conceive clearly, and one that can be held only under cover of half-thoughts and cant phrases. Perception carves out its conventional units, and final causes insinuate themselves into the survey of facts, when their patient genesis is ignored or untraceable. Life on the whole is a proof of the possibility of life; each sort of life is a proof that circumstances made that sort of life inevitable. A vigorous and courageous animal assumes that fortune will not fail him. Did he not assume it, how should he be able to live? This sense of safety may be expressed and justified intellectually by finding the facts or habits of nature which support our own habits, and so bring the customary values about in the round of our experience. If these favouring circumstances are dominant in our world we shall be as safe in fact as we feel ourselves to be by instinct. This situation might then be expressed elliptically, by saying that the good is certain to prevail, or that values are powers: the justification for such an expression being that our assurance of safety and good fortune rests on a substantial harmony between our interests and our circumstances. But when this harmony becomes audible, when for a moment some value is realized, all potentiality and material efficacy are left far behind: we are in the realm of actuality, of music, of spirit; and the value actualized lives and ends in itself. The promise which often lies in it, as well as the disillusion or disaster that may ensue, will not be due to that value in its moral nature, to that living and immaterial good; it will be due to the organization of nature beneath. All moral functions have their material organs and their material effects; in that context they are powers, or rather vehicles of power—for as the Moslems say, there is no power but Allah. Goods are, in their material ground, an integral part of the flux of events; and the healthy habit in nature which creates them once may repeat them and perfect them, if the season is favourable and the fates allow.

III

FOR my purpose, however, it is fortunately unimportant to dispel these ambiguities, dear to half-hearted philosophies, because the Platonic doctrine at least is clear. If for the Platonist goods and evils are everlastingly fixed and distinct, this moral dogmatism in him is no accident of temperament, no mere lack of moral elasticity, as in the bigot. If he is sure that some goods often passionately loved are nevertheless false goods, it is only because he attributes a definite and unchangeable constitution to the material world and to human nature. Life, he thinks, has been kindled and is alone sustained by the influence of pre-existing celestial models. It is by imitating these models in some measure that we exist at all, and only in imitating, loving, and contemplating them that we can ever be happy. They are our good. In themselves, however, they are inviolate beings, serenely shedding, like the stars, an everlasting radiance, and no doubt happy beings, if they are living and self-contemplative: but they are by no means mere goals which this nether world sets freely for itself, or perfections which it might enjoy intrinsically. God and the Ideas could be ruling powers, because they were existing

9

beings, definite in their character and influence. They exercised a miraculous, magnetic control over formless matter, inducing in it here and there an inward striving to imitate their forms. They therefore had the greatest value for the creature whose life was directed upon them and who invincibly loved them; but this value in them remained relative to the aspiration of their lover, and variable in so far as his nature might change; so that St. Thomas Aquinas goes so far as to say that to the sinner God becomes an evil—the Christian God, he means, for I suppose the reprobate might still find a divine friend in Bacchus or Venus. It was never the actual values found in the world that were separated from it, either in Platonism or in Christianity, and conceived to compose an eternal world behind it. The powers that were creative, substantial, and permanent were not values at all, but the *underpinning* which values required if they were to arise; and although this substructure had to be in itself physical or metaphysical, the discovery of it had momentous consequences for morals, in that it enabled the enlightened believer to distinguish possible attainable goods from the impossible happiness after which the heathen seek. Those goods which the nature of things or the will of God assures and sanctions are the " eternal values "; the others are " the current valuations of the worldling." Thus religion or philosophy was the great arbiter of true values, the guide of life; it justified the sense of sin and the hope of salvation. The distinction between true goods and false goods can never be established by ignorant feeling or by conscience not backed by a dogmatic view of the facts: for felt values, taken absolutely and regarded as unconditioned, are all equally genuine in their excellence, and equally momentary in their existence. The distinction hangs on the system of forces, natural or supernatural, believed to produce and sustain these various goods, some for a moment, others for ever. *Some* constitution the cosmos must have, and must disclose to our faith or science, if ever we are to decide which of our pleasures or affections reveal " the unseen and eternal world behind," and which of them threaten to conceal it.

IV

THIS separation of the Platonic Ideas from the things which manifested them has been much blamed, yet it goes with another doctrine which is much prized, often by the same critics. The precious consequence of this abhorred dualism was that the Ideas, if separate, might be powers, creative forces that generated their expressions. Separation is a pre-requisite to causal connection: a thing cannot be derived from a part of itself. If Ideas were only values, if they were immanent in things, as the form of a poem or its peculiar beauty is immanent in that poem, there would be no sense in saying that the beauty or the form was a power that had produced the poem. Not only would each be dead without the other, as Dean Inge says, but each would be nothing; the poem arises by taking that form, and the form is merely that precise arrangement of words and images. The beauty of a thing is an essence which it manifests spontaneously, a pure quality of being revealed there, and perhaps never to be revealed again. The natural causes that produce the thing and bring it to notice produce also this manifestation of beauty in it; both spring into existence together out of a complex of circumstances and impulses among which it is impossible to place that homeless essence, the form of beauty thereby revealed; yet this form is their only value for the spirit, a value which that precise conjunction of causes was needed to realize.

There is a sense—a somewhat esoteric sense —in which such essences as beauty may be called " the most real things in the universe." They are the ultimate characters by which one thing can be distinguished from another in the flux of nature, or one thought from another in the mind; and if the word " real " be used sentimentally, to mean whatever is most clear or important or nearest to the heart, such values will be not only " most real " but even the only " reality," because their presence or absence, their purity or contradiction, make up the spiritual sum of life, all that matters in it, without which no one would care to raise his head from the pillow of non-being. If, however, by " most real " we understand most primitive or fundamental physically, the roots of existence, it is clearly impossible that the most real things should be values. Values presuppose living beings having a direction of development, and exerting themselves in it, so that good and evil may exist in reference to them. That the good should be relative to actual natures and simply their innate ideal, latent or realized, is essential to its being truly a good. Otherwise the term " good " would be an empty title applied to some existing object or force for no assignable reason.

The good may nevertheless be called absolute in several senses proper to current speech. The good is by no means relative to opinion, but is rooted in the unconscious and fatal nature of living beings, a nature which pre-determines for them the difference between foods and poisons, happiness and misery. The moralist may speak for others with authority when he knows them better than they know themselves, but not otherwise. Moreover, their natural good may be absolute in the sense of being fixed and unalterable, so long as the living beings concerned and the circumstances in which they flourish remain constant in type. That human nature and the world are un-changeable was an assumption of classic times which survives often in modern moralists, without its dogmatic justification. Finally, the good may be called absolute in the sense of being single and all-sufficient, filling the whole heart, and leaving nothing in the rest of the universe in the least tempting, inter-esting, or worth distinguishing. It is in this sense that lovers and mystics proclaim the absoluteness of the good with which they are united, and when the thing is true as a con-fession it would be frivolous and ungracious to quarrel with it as a dogma.

V

If then the Ideas were immanent in things, as the beauty of a poem is immanent in it, they could not conceivably be powers producing their occasional manifestation. The beauties *intrinsic* to the tragedy of Hamlet could not have caused Shakespeare to compose that play since those values could not possibly come to existence until the play had already composed itself in his fancy, and burst into just those beauties. In order to maintain seriously the efficacy of Ideas and to conceive matters in the orthodox Platonic way, we must make a different supposition. Suppose Hamlet had been a living prince, like the present Prince of Wales, and that Shakespeare, with his company of players, had happened to appear at this prince's court, and had conceived for him a passionate Platonic attachment, such as he seems to have conceived for the W.H. of the Sonnets: and suppose further that, by the prodigious inspiration of this passion, Shakespeare had been led to imagine episodes and phrases that might in part express so tender, intellectual, and profound a character as that living Prince seemed to him to possess; then indeed a most real Hamlet, with a pre-existing power and charm, might have been the " only begetter " of the play. In exactly this way the Platonic Ideas, the Christian God, or the Christ of devout Christians, may be conceived to be the causes of their temporal manifestations in matter or in the souls of men. Evidently a play written in such circumstances might have the same intrinsic value as one purely imaginary; but it would not be this literary value that would constitute the model or the creative influence which had produced the play; this literary value would have been begotten, like the play itself and inseparably from it, by the influence radiating from the living Hamlet, a prince having his existence apart, who by chance had come for a moment within the poet's orbit.

This separation between the creator and the created is not only the condition of derivation, contact, and causal influence, but it is also the condition of a genuine worship; because then that which is expression in the poet is at the same time homage in the lover, as it could not be except fatuously and by a poetic affectation if the being loved did not exist separately. And " only begetter " is the right phrase to indicate the relation between such a creative influence and its work. A Platonic Idea could never be the whole cause of its temporal expressions; a material or feminine element is involved that may receive that influence and make it fruitful; a fact which would also explain the many variants and the many imperfections which things might exhibit in response to the same unchanging virtue of their divine model.

When the matter is so conceived all force departs from the contention that if we separate God or the Ideas from the temporal world, "both are dead." God and the Ideas, like the living Prince Hamlet, would remain exactly as they were, with all their intrinsic warmth and virtue; and the temporal world, like the Shakespearean tragedy, would also remain just as it is, with all its literary values. The only difference would be that the living prince would have inspired no poet, and that the self-inspired poet would have celebrated no living prince. Shakespeare's Hamlet would be reduced to what, in fact, he is, an object of occasional imagination, a pure essence, and not a power. Meantime the inexhaustible powers which, if a divine life existed, would certainly lie in it, would have continued to radiate unmanifested, like those many rays of the sun which are dissipated in space, not being by chance reflected or absorbed and made temporally fruitful by any speck of an earth.

Platonism accordingly would be entirely stultified and eviscerated if it were not suffered to be all that modern criticism, inspired as it is by a subjective and psychological philosophy, most thoroughly dislikes; I mean, supernaturalistic, realistic, and dualistic. This is only another way of saying that, according to the Platonic doctrine, God and the unseen world really exist in themselves, so that they can precede, create, attract, and survive their earthly emanations.

VI

Is this to say that Aristotle and all the other critics of Platonism have had no reason on their side? Far from it: their criticism was amply justified by the facts of nature, and their only defect was perhaps not to have felt its full force, and to have still attributed power to those very Ideas to which they denied separate existence.[1] The Platonic system is mythological: if taken literally and dogmatically, it can seem to cold reason nothing but a gratuitous fiction, as all systems of religion or metaphysics necessarily seem to the outsider. Of course they are not inwardly gratuitous; they are the fervent expression and product of the deepest minds; and anyone capable of sharing the inspiration which prompted them will know them to be inevitable, persuasive, and morally coherent. Thus Dean Inge says that those who think Platonism dualistic have simply not understood; that is (if I myself understand him), they have not understood it from within, genetically, historically, emotionally; they have not recovered the experience

---

[1] I have elsewhere ventured to suggest that perhaps Aristotle himself was not guilty of this inconsistency. Cf. *Dialogues in Limbo: the Secret of Aristotle*, pp. 181-193.

and the immanent logic which, as a matter of fact, held the Platonic dualism in solution. This dualism appears only in the dogma precipitated and left, as it were, as a sediment; and the most sympathetic modern critic can hardly take such dogma seriously. He cannot receive it as a revelation, like a humble catechumen, drinking-in the marvellous supernatural facts from the lips of the masters. Platonism, like Christianity, cannot now produce in him the illusion which it was its early mission to produce. When he turns back to the origin of such a faith, he cannot, for all his sympathy, share the prophetic impulse which carried the Fathers from their first intuitions to the full expression of the same in consistent and final dogmas. Truth for him means historical, psychological truth; and the whole force of his learning and imagination is spent in dissolving those dogmas dramatically into their subjective components, and showing them to be but verbal expressions for certain radical ambient values. This is what, in fact, they were, or something of that kind: and he may be assured of this not merely by the naturalistic philosophy (perhaps unconsciously inspiring him) which proclaims such dogmas to be nothing else, but by the study of the surviving documents. Plato's writings in particular show clearly that the eventual Platonic system was but a moral and poetic fable.

The Ideas originally were really nothing but values. Socrates had conceived them as forms of the good, and this good itself was identical with the useful, beneficent, or advantageous. In the *Republic* we learn that anything—a shepherd or a ruler, a bridle or a bed—is good when it fulfils its natural function. Fitness to control a horse for the purposes of war, commerce, or sport would be the Idea (or value) of a bridle, and fitness to induce sound and comfortable sleep would be, I suppose, the Idea of a bed; and as to the eternal Idea of a ruler or shepherd, what should it be but to protect and conduct his sheep or his people, and in due season to shear them? This homely Socratic wisdom may seem not far removed from " the current valuations of the worldling "; it rested on no revelation, private or public, and had no principle save the reasonableness of the simplest mortal when forced by shrewd questions to disentangle his prejudices and to discover what he really wants. But great is the power of logic, when the mind is single and the heart open. In a trice it will bring the humblest judgements into the clarifying presence of the highest good. Socrates was a plain man, but fearless; he was omnivorous, playful, ironical, but absolutely determined. His one purpose was to be rational, to find and do what was best. If Anaxagoras would tell him what profit men might draw from the sun and moon,

he would listen gladly; but if it was only a
question of the substance or motions of those
bodies, he would turn his back on Anaxagoras
and laugh. This cobbler's wisdom was the
same that almost made saints of the Cynics; it
reappeared in the monks; it may reappear any
day in some popular prophet. A fervid
utilitarianism has a strangely revolutionary
force: in squeezing the world to get every drop
of pure good out of it, it leaves the world
worthless, and has to throw it away: nothing
remains but the immediate good of the spirit,
the naked soul longing to be saved.

VII

In Plato and in his followers this revolution
took more time and a larger sweep. Plato's
mind was more accomplished and less conse-
crated than that of his master: that of his
followers was more dogmatic and single than
his own. Idealism, as it moves away from its
origins, may easily become idolatrous: while
leaving earthly things dry and empty, it may
worship the pure forms which these things
would have had if they had been perfect. In
criticizing and condemning this world the
prophet will find himself in the presence of
another world, its sublimated image. The gift
of thinking in myths, once native to the Greeks,
was not altogether lost; it could still fuse the
forms seen with a life unseen; it could trans-
form definition of terms into intuition of
Ideas; it could personify the functions of
things and turn their virtues into patron
deities animating those things and causing
them to shine with a strength and beauty alien
to their earthly substance. In the unclouded,
synthetic, believing mind of Plotinus this
chastened mythology crystallized into the
most beautiful of systems.

An inexhaustible divine energy—so the
system ran—poured perpetually down into the

chaos of matter, animating and shaping it as well as that torpid substance would permit. At the bottom or centre there was little life, but it stirred more actively and nobly at each successive level, somewhat as the light of the sun floods the ether absolutely, the air variously, the sea dubiously, and the earth only darkly, with a shallow warmth. Hence the hierarchy of created goods, which is itself a good; and as to the defeats and confusions involved in being other than the highest, and other than one's own Idea, they were due to the inopportune inertia of matter, or to blind accident, or to a diabolical soul intervening and poisoning the fountains of divine grace. All levels of being were good in some measure, each after its kind. Consistently, and yet perhaps only with an effort and against the spirit of his times, Plotinus defended the excellence of the material world against the Gnostics, and the worthiness of the state and of the traditions of Hellenism, so that an emperor and even an empress might be his auditors without offence; and his philosophy remained Socratic in principle, a mythical underpinning to morals, and not a view of nature founded on observation, like those of the Stoics and the Epicureans. Yet in the five or six hundred years since Socrates, moral life itself had changed its centre. The good of the soul and her salvation had taken the place of domestic, military, and political goods; so that while the various spheres of being, like the terraces of Dante's Purgatorio, were all permanent and divinely appointed, the spirit now moved through them without rest. Its abiding-place was beyond. They were but the rounds of a Jacob's ladder by which the soul might climb again to her native heaven, and it was only " *there*," above, that she truly lived and had been blessed from all eternity.

Platonism, as Dean Inge observes, has no tendency to become pantheistic. Its first principle is the difference between good and evil. Its final dogmas describe a half-astronomical, half-dramatic setting for the phases of spiritual life. The divine spirit burned with such an intense and concentrated fire, it was so rich in its inner being, it overflowed into a celestial hierarchy of so many choirs, all superior to man, even on earth it found so many marvellous and amiable non-human manifestations, that man, with his two-footed featherlessness and his political artifices, lost his ancient Hellenic dignity: it was almost a disgrace for the soul to be expressed in a body or a body in a statue. Thus the imagined universe which was to shelter morality threatened to outgrow its original office. Man and his earthly fortunes began to seem to the contemplative mind but incidents in the barnyard. The only ambition worthy of a philosopher was to transcend and transfigure his human nature, and to pass unsullied through this nether world in adoration of the world above.

VIII

PLOTINUS professed to be, and actually was, an orthodox Platonist; and yet this dominant sense in him of the spiritual life was perfectly foreign to Socrates and Plato. I say this without forgetting the dialogues on love or the almost Roman religiosity of the *Laws*. After having been very poetical Plato became very austere; but his philosophy remained political to the end. To this descendant of Solon the universe could never be anything but a crystal case to hold the jewel of a Greek city. Divine as the heavens were, they were but a mothering and brooding power: in their refined materiality and mathematical divinity they circled about the earth, at once vivifying it and rebuking it by the visible presence of an exemplary good. The notion of the heavenly spheres was no mere optical image, the dream of a philosopher who, on a clear night, could measure the radius of the universe with the naked eye: this image was a moral parable. The realm of ethics will always be a set of concentric circles. Life necessarily radiates from centres; it stirs here, in the self; from here it looks abroad for supports and extensions, in the family, the nation, the intellectual world, the parent and subject universe. Wide as it may seem, this

27

prospect is homely, and taken from the hearth of Vesta.

If the theology of Socrates and Plato was in this way domestic, the remnant of traditional religion in them was doubly so. Their attachment to ancient piety was childlike and superstitious when it remained personal, but more often it was expressly political and politic: they saw in religion a ready means of silencing dangerous questions and rebuking wickedness. It was a matter of moral education and police, and in no sense spiritual.

As to the Socratic philosophy of love, there is an obvious spiritual tendency in it, inasmuch as it bids the heart turn from the temporal to the eternal; and it does so not by way of an arid logic but by a true discipline of the affections, sublimating erotic passion into a just enthusiasm for all things beautiful and perfect. This is the secret of Platonism, which makes it perennial, so that if it were ever lost as a tradition it would presently be revived as an inspiration. It lives by a poignant sense of eternal values—the beautiful and the good— revealed for a moment in living creatures or in earthly harmonies. Yet who has not felt that this Platonic enthusiasm is somewhat equivocal and vain? Why? Because its renunciation is not radical. In surrendering some particular hope or some personal object of passion, it preserves and feeds the passion itself; there is no true catharsis, no liberation, but a sort of substitution and subterfuge, often hypocritical. Pure spiritual life cannot be something compensatory, a consolation for having missed more solid satisfactions: it should be rather the flower of all satisfactions, in which satisfaction becomes free from care, selfless, wholly actual and, in that inward sense, eternal. Spiritual life is simple and direct, but it is intellectual. Love, on the contrary, as Plotinus says, is something material, based on craving and a sense of want. For this reason the beautiful and the good, for the Platonic enthusiast, remain urgent values; he would cease to be a true Platonist or a rapt lover if he *understood*, if he discounted his illusions, rose above the animal need or the mental prejudice which made those values urgent, and relegated them to their relative station, where by their nature they belong. Yet this is what a pure spirit would do, one truly emancipated and enlightened.

IX

HERE, at the risk of parting company with Dean Inge and even with Plato, I come to a radical conclusion. Spiritual life is not a worship of " values," whether found in things or hypostatized into supernatural powers. It is the exact opposite; it is *disintoxication* from their influence. Not that spiritual insight can ever remove values from nature or cease to feel them in their moral black and white and in all their aesthetic iridescence. Spirit knows these vital necessities: it has been quickened in their bosom. All animals have within them a principle by which to distinguish good from evil, since their existence and welfare are furthered by some circumstances and acts and are hindered by others. Self-knowledge, with a little experience of the world, will then easily set up the Socratic standard of values natural and inevitable to any man or to any society. These values each society will disentangle in proportion to its intelligence and will defend in proportion to its vitality. But who would dream that *spiritual life* was at all concerned in asserting these human and local values to be alone valid, or in supposing that they were especially divine, or bound to dominate the universe for ever?

In fact, the great masters of the spiritual life are evidently not the Greeks, not even the Alexandrian Greeks, but the Indians, their disciples elsewhere in the East, and those Moslems, Christians, and Jews who have surrendered precisely that early, unregenerate claim to be enveloped in a protecting world designed for their benefit or vindication, a claim of which Platonism after all was but a refined version. To cling to familiar treasures and affections is human, but it is not particularly spiritual; to hypostatize these home values into a cosmic system especially planned to guarantee them, certainly expresses an intelligible passionate need for comfort and coddling in the universe, but with spirituality it has nothing to do. If such confidence may be called faith, it may also be called fatuity and insolence; an insolence innocent in a spirited child, but out of place in a philosopher. Spirituality comes precisely of surrendering this animal arrogance and this moral fanaticism and substituting for them pure intelligence: not a discoursing cleverness or scepticism, but perfect candour and impartial vision. Spirit is merciful and tender because it has no private motive to make it spiteful; yet it is unflinchingly austere because it cannot make any private motive its own. It need have no scientific or artistic pretensions; it appears quite adequately in straight seeing of simple things; these, to pure spirit, are speculative enough and good to whet its edge upon; the proudest dreams of science or theology are no better for the purpose. The spirit is content with the widow's mite and a cup of cold water; it considers the lilies of the field; it can say with literal truth: Inasmuch as ye did it unto the least of these, ye did it unto me.

As the spirit is no respecter of persons, so it is no respecter of worlds: it is willing to put up with any of them, to be feasted in one or to be martyred in another. And while it is allowed to live—a point that concerns the world it lives in rather than the spirit itself—it looks with a clear and untroubled sympathy on such manifestations of being as happen to be unrolled before it. As it loves the non-human parts of nature, so it loves the human parts, and is in no way hostile to the natural passions and to the political and religious institutions that happen to prevail. If spirit was to be incarnate and to appear in existence at all, it had to be born in one odd world or another: why should it quarrel with its earthly cradle? This is not to say that all circumstances are equally favourable to the spiritual life. On the contrary, most circumstances exclude it altogether; the vast abysses of nature seem to be uninhabited; and even where spirit feebly appears, it is in order to be, very often, stifled at once, or long tormented. Almost always its world is too much with it; the spirit is so deeply engaged and distracted by current events that it cannot realize its proper function, which is to see such things as come in its way under the form of eternity, in their intrinsic character and relative value, in their transitiveness and necessity, in a word, in their truth. This contemplative habit evidently finds a freer course in solitude than in society, in art than in business, in prayer than in argument. It is stimulated by beautiful and constant things more than by things ugly, tedious, crowded, or uncertain. For this reason it is more prevalent and freer in the East than in the West, among Catholics than among Protestants, among Moslems than among Jews. For the same reason the Platonic system, up to a certain point, is sympathetic to the spirit. Its universe was compact and immortal; the oscillations of fortune on earth could not disturb its unchangeable order. If nature were conceived to be, as in fact she is, barbarous and in indefinite flux, giving rein to anything and everything, there would seem hardly to be time to reach perfection on any level of being before the soil was undermined and the budding Idea was lost and dissipated. The great merit of an unchanging world is that all its inhabitants can be adapted to it. If they ever fall out of tune the cause will be but a passing disease and an accidental slackness in the strings; it will be easy to screw up the pegs, to renew a snapped cord, and to restore the harmony. Such a world offers an immovable basis and sanction for the good: it establishes an orthodox morality. Imperfection enters it only below the circle of the moon, like bad manners below stairs; and even here, on earth, evil is but an oscillation and dizziness in matter which nature perpetually calls back to the norm, as the motion of a top rights it in its gyrations.

X

I AM not confident, however, that a pure spirit would feel safe in such a seven-walled celestial castle, or would prize the sort of safety which, if it were real, it would afford. Existence is contingent essentially. As things might just as well have been different, so they might just as well prove to be inconstant; and since they cannot manifest their groundlessness by now being other than they happen to be, they may manifest it by being other at other times and places. No existing being can have the means of knowing that it will always exist or prosper in the universe: the neatest cosmos and the most solitary god might collide with something unsuspected; or the unsuspected thing might exist in its own preserves without being discovered or coming into collision. Yet that undiscovered world, for the spirit, would be as real and as interesting as this world. Ignorance cannot justify any negative prophecy: but existence, while it is the home of particular certitudes, is also a cage in which an inevitable and infinite ignorance sings and dies imprisoned. Existence is self-centred, limited in character by the character which it chances to have, and in duration by the crawling fact that it exists while it is found existing. There is no necessary and all-comprehensive being except the realm of essence, to which existence is irrelevant: for whether the whole exist or only a part, or even if no part existed, the alternative fact would always be knocking at the door; and nothing in the actual facts could ever prove that the door would not suddenly open and let the contrary in. Like people living on the slopes of volcanoes, we ignore these possibilities, although a catastrophe is rapidly approaching each of us in the form of death, and who knows how soon it may overtake the whole confused life of our planet? Nevertheless, except in the interests of detachment and freedom, spirit has no reason for dwelling on other possible worlds. Would any of them be less contingent than this one, or nearer to the heart of infinite Being? And would not any of them, whatever its character, lead the spirit inexorably *there*? To master the actual is the best way of transcending it. Those who know but one language, like the Greeks, seem to find language a purer and more transparent vehicle than those of us who notice its idiosyncrasies and become entangled in its meshes. So it is the saints most steeped each in his traditional religion who are nearest together in spirit; and if nature caused them to change places, it is they that, after a moment's pause to get their bearings, would be most at ease in one another's skins. No one is

more unspiritual than a heretic, or more grace-
less and wretched than an unfrocked priest;
yet the frock of the faithful is but an earthly
garment; it melts into the clouds which, in
their ascension, they leave behind them.

XI

IN what places the spirit shall awake, and how long and how freely it shall be suffered to flourish are evidently questions of mundane physics and politics: it is the world's business to call down spirit to dwell in it, not the spirit's business to make a world in which to dwell. The friends of spirit, in their political capacity, will of course defend those forms of society in which, given their particular race and traditions, spirit may best exist: they will protect it in whatever organs and instruments it may already have appeared, and will take care that it pursues its contemplative life undisturbed in its ancient sanctuaries. Spirituality has material conditions; not only the general conditions of life and intuition (for a man must exist before he can become a spiritual man), but subtler and more special conditions such as concentration of thought, indifference to fortune and reputation, warmth of temperament (because spirit cannot burn clear except at a high temperature) disciplined into chastity and renunciation. These and other such conditions the master of novices does well to consider; but spirit itself, when once aroused, does not look back in that direction. Many Christian saints have qualified their spirituality with too much self-consciousness; it was no doubt their religious duty to examine their consciences and study to advance in holiness; but the holiness really did not begin until they forgot themselves in the thought of God. So with those who were consumed with zeal for the Church, the conversion of sinners, and other works of charity. These are moral interests or duties accruing to men as members of some particular society; they are political cares. They may be accompanied by spiritual insight, if it be really salvation or spiritualization of souls that preoccupies the missionary, and not some outward change of habit or allegiance, that may make other people more like himself and ensure the dominance of his home traditions. Political zeal even in the true friends of spirit is not spiritual; a successful apostle must have rather a worldly mind, because he needs to have his hand on the pulse of the world; his appeal would not be intelligible if it were not threatening or spectacular or full of lewd promises. It will be only afterwards, perhaps, when people have been domesticated in the new faith, that the spirit will descend upon them. The spirit itself is not afraid of being stamped out here, or anxious to be kindled there; its concern is not about its instances or manifestations; it is not essentially learned or social; its kingdom is not of this world. It leaves propaganda to those who call themselves its friends but probably know nothing of it, or are even its enemies, and only the agents of some worldly transformation ultimately quite nugatory.

Nor has the world, on its side, any obligation to cultivate the spiritual life. Obligations are moral; they presuppose a physical and social organism with immanent spontaneous interests which may impose those obligations. The value and opportuneness of spiritual life, in any of its possible forms, must be adjudged by reason in view of the moral economy for which, in any instance, reason may speak. All values fall within the purview of ethics, which is a part of politics. Spirituality is the supreme good for those who are called to it, the few whose intellectual thirst can be quenched only by impartial truth and the self-annihilating contemplation of all Being. The statesman and the father of a family may not always welcome this disposition; it may seem to them wasteful and idle. Just as the value of an artist must be judged by the world, in view of all the interests which his art affects or subserves, while the artist himself lives only in his own labour, irresponsible, technical, and visionary; so the value of spiritual life in general, or in any of its incidental forms, must be judged morally by the world, in view of its own ambitions, while the spirit, standing invisibly at its elbow, judges the world and its ambitions spiritually.

XII

I<small>T</small> is impossible that spirit in a living creature should ever be wholly freed from the body and from the world; for in its inwardness it would have ceased to follow and enact the fortunes of that creature; it would either have been absorbed in the contemplation of pure Being and become virtually omniscient, or at least it would contemplate its special objects equably under the form of eternity, and not in the perspectives determined by the station of its body in time and place. Pure Being, or these special essences and truths, would evidently gain nothing by the fact that this new mind had been lost in them; and this mind, in gaining them, would have lost itself; it would, in fact, have ceased to exist separately. Meantime the body of that creature might go on living automatically; the mind which it had previously fed, as a lamp feeds its flame, would have evaporated, gone up into the sun, and ceased to light the precincts and penumbra of that particular vessel, or to be a measure of its little oil. But a living automaton is by nature conscious: the lamp has not been materially extinguished: the creature is accordingly still breeding a faithful if flickering mind, which feels and notes its further vicissitudes. Evi-

dently this fresh mind is the true continuation
of that creature's experience; it is again con-
tinuously cognizant of that body in that world.
The effort to liberate souls from their bodies
or to transport them beyond their world has
therefore a rather ironical result : the redeemed
soul ceases to be anybody's soul, and the body
continues to have a soul that is quite personal
and unregenerate.

The difference between the life of the spirit
and that of the flesh is itself a spiritual difference : the two are not to be divided materially
or in their occasions and themes so much as in
the quality of their attention : the one is
anxiety, inquiry, desire, and fear ; the other is
intuitive possession. The spirit is not a tale-
bearer having a mock world of its own to
substitute for the humble circumstances of this
life ; it is only the faculty—the disenchanting
and re-enchanting faculty—of seeing this world
in its simple truth. Therefore all the worldly
hatred of spirit—and it is very fierce—can
never remove the danger that, after a thousand
persecutions and a long conspiracy of derision,
a child of the spirit should be born in the
bosom of the worldly family. The more
organic and perfect the life of the world becomes, the more intelligent it will be : and what
shall prevent intelligence from asking what all
this pother is about and driving the money-
changers from the house of prayer? Spirit

must have some organ; but when once aroused it does not look in the direction of its organ or care at all about preserving it. It looks rather, as we see in Indian philosophy, to a realm anterior to all worlds, and finds there a comprehensive object which in one sense includes all worlds, since it is infinite Being, but for that very reason excludes the enacted existence of any one of them, since they can be enacted, as the moments of time are enacted, only by excluding and ousting one another. *This* world, for a speculative mind, is exactly analogous to *this* moment. It seems alone real to those who inhabit it, but its pre-eminence is relative and egotistical: if maintained dogmatically it becomes at once illusory and absurd.

XIII

NOT that the existence of a particular world—
perhaps its exclusive existence—is an evil. If
the lovers of pure Being are ever tempted to
say so, it is only in their human capacity,
because some rude fact may have wounded
their feelings. These feelings are a part of the
world which they condemn, inevitable as this
world is inevitable, and unnecessary in the
sense in which this world is unnecessary. The
contradiction or self-dislike which they betray
in that world is, no doubt, a defect from the
point of view of the parts in it which are
quarrelling, each of which would wish to have
it all its own way. But this fact does not
render that world, or the conflicts in it, evil
absolutely. Evil can arise only within each
world when it becomes faithless to some Idea
which it has begun to pursue, or is crossed in
the pursuit of it either by some external enemy
(if any) or by the inward contradiction and
complexity of its impulses, which allow it only
to drift towards uncertain, tragic, and romantic
issues. But, as we see in some desperately
romantic philosophers, this very disorder may
please an imagination which is stirred by that
stimulus more deeply than by any impulse
towards harmony and fixity of form. Some

impulse towards form, some initial essence or essences, a world must preserve so long as it exists, else it would dissolve into chaos or into that metaphysical non-entity, matter without form: but this modicum of form may be composed by the perpetual defeat of every particular endeavour, and the greatest evil of the greatest number of souls may fulfil the romantic ideal. The theologians who have maintained that the damnation of the great majority is no evil in the sight of God, and leaves his intrinsic holiness and glory unsullied, have understood the matter speculatively; and although the ferocity of the Calvinists was not spiritual, and their notion of " an angry God " was grotesque, there was spirituality in their elevation above the weak judgements of the flesh and even of the heart; only that the speculative sword really cuts both ways, and their sense for the superhuman should also have dissolved their moral fanaticism. Pure Being is infinite, its essence includes all essences; how then should it issue particular commands, or be an acrimonious moralist?

The two-edged sword falls again here. If it be true that the world can be evil only in its own eyes and therefore only partially and pro-visionally, until the eyes are closed or are hardened like the eagle's to that wounding light, so it is true also that it can be good in its own eyes only: and more, that the spiritual

life and the pure Being to which its contemplation is addressed, can be good only in relation
to the living souls that may find their good
there. Plotinus and many other mystics have
admitted that the One, though habitually
called good, is not properly so called. It is the
good of religion, because religion is a conversion
from one object of pursuit to another, under
the form of the good : but in the One itself, or
in attainment, the pursuit is absent, and the
category of the good no longer has any applica-
tion. The title may be retained, in human
parlance, to indicate that the attainment
really satisfies the aspiration which preceded,
and does not disappoint it; for to end there,
to end absolutely, was the very aim of that
aspiration. The case is like that of a man
building his tomb, or bequeathing his property
to his son ; the result is a good for him in that
he desired it, but not in that he survives to
enjoy it. So is the peace that passeth understanding, that annuls desire, and that excludes
the gasping consciousness of peace.

XIV

SPIRIT, which is ultimately addressed to pure Being, is not itself this pure Being. It is the gift of intuition, feeling, or apprehension: an overtone of animal life, a realization, on a hypostatic plane, of certain moving unities in matter. So, at least, I understand the word; but its original meaning was a breath or wind, and hence, often, an influence. In this last sense it is used in Christian theology; the Holy Ghost is not the Father nor the Son, but proceeds from them and animates the world, or at least the souls of the elect. It is the fountain of grace. We also read in the gospel that God is a spirit, to be worshipped in spirit and in truth. Here the word evidently bears more than one sense; the spirit in which God is worshipped is a disposition of the mind, whereas God himself, we may presume, is a spirit in the mighty sense in which Jehovah swept the void, a breath or a word, bringing order out of chaos; the same voice that spoke to Job out of the whirlwind, with the sheer authority of power. Spirit thus seems to be sometimes a

47

creative energy, sometimes a sanctifying influence. So in the Latin hymn:

Veni creator Spiritus
corda tuorum visitans
imple supernâ gratiâ
quae tu creasti pectora.

This double function of spirit, if we investigated its origin, would bring back the double source of Christian doctrine, here Hebraic and there Platonic: a profound dualism which custom scarcely avails to disguise or theology to heal. Creative power and redeeming grace point in opposite directions; but a complete religion needs to look both ways, feeding piously at the breast of nature, yet weaning itself spiritually from that necessary comfort to the contemplation of superhuman and eternal things. The object of piety is necessity, power, the laws of life and prosperity, and to call these things spirit is pure mythology; they are indeed a great wind, sometimes balmy, sometimes terrible; and it is the part of wisdom to take shelter from it, or spread wings or sails in it, according as it lists to blow. But to what end? To live, to have spirit, to understand all these things.

There is also a conventional modern sense in which we speak of the spirit of an age, a place, or a book, meaning some vague tendency or inspiration either actually dominating that thing or suggested by it to the mind of a third

person. This is a verbal survival of myth,
poetry become cant: spirit here means those
characters of a thing which a myth-making
mind would have attributed to a spirit.

In contrast to all these uses I am employing
the word spirit to mean something actual;
indeed, the very fact of actuality, the gleam
of intuition or feeling. But this gleam ordin-
arily serves only to light up material life and
the perspectives in which it moves in time and
in space: an incessant sketchy sense of the
affairs of the body and of its world. The
digestion and preparation of action (as the
behaviourists have shown) is a physical matter.
In that business the spirit is entirely superfluous.
The behaviourists even affect to deny its
existence, on the ground that it is invisible and
would be a useless luxury in nature: excellent
economy, as if a man, the better to provide for
his future, should starve himself to death.
The spirit in us is that which, morally, we
actually are: if anything is to be expunged
from the complex face of reality it might
rather be our material and social setting and
all the strange and incoherent stories told us in
history and science. Certainly all these appar-
ent or reported facts would be perfectly vain,
if they did not create the spirit, and teach it
to observe and enjoy them. So we are brought
back to the immediate revelation of things,
which is also their ultimate value: we are

E

brought back to the spirit. Its life is composed
of feelings and intuitions, in many stages and
degrees; and when spirit is free and collected
it has no life but this spiritual life, in which the
ultimate is immediate. All the experiences of
the spirit, until they are so exorcized and
appropriated—so enshrined in pure Being—are
sheer distraction.

XV

WERE any world perfect, as the Platonists thought that this world was in its upper parts, its spirit would view it with the same contemplative satisfaction with which it views any pure essence that spontaneously engages its attention. It would not, in respect to that perfect world, be harassed by remorse, as it must be in an imperfect world when it counts the cost of existence and considers the dreadful sufferings which plagued it like a nightmare, before something beautiful and good could appear even for a moment. I say *remorse*, because such is the feeling that comes over me when I remember the travail which, at least in man, the spirit has had to endure in bringing its better life to birth: but the spirit itself has no guilt in the matter; it was caught in a vice; and it may accept and overlook that terrible gestation when at last it reaches the open and rewards itself with an hour of freedom and gladness. These are its natural notes: it is born out of an achieved harmony, only in creatures already formed and in some measure fit to live: contradiction and torment are inexplicable to it, and danger a cause of laughter. How should spirit, the very essence of radiance, ever become morose? It runs and

51

sparkles wherever it may, the free child of nature. It has no grudge against its fostering world; on the contrary, nothing but delighted wonder. It has no native enmity towards the flesh—that comes to it afterwards from the sad flesh itself; it has no disinclination to folly. The difference between folly and wisdom, between crime and piety, is not naturally known to spirit; it is a lesson learned by experience, in view of the conditions of material life; spirit would of itself gladly take a turn with the devil, who is also a spirit. Yet all this innocent joy and courage native to spirit bind it to the world with no tie. That which is tied, that which cannot live save in its home climate and family nest, is only the mortal psyche, the poor, absurd, accidental human person. The psyche in each of us is like Vesta, the goddess of the Hearth, mother of the Promethean flame, mother of spirit; and she needs to learn the difficult unselfishness of the parent—or of the foster-parent: for her child is of another race. She must be content to be abandoned, revisited only in haste on some idle holiday, with a retrospective piety; and even as she embraces her full-grown over-topping son he will seem a stranger to her, and she will catch sight of his eyes, gazing over her head into a far country.

At the same time this homelessness of spirit is not romantic; it is not impatience of this and longing for that; it is not the snobbery of learning and culture so characteristic of intellectual people who are not spiritual. No: the homelessness of spirit comes from detachment, detachment no less from the grander thing which the snob respects and pretends to know as from this humbler thing which he despises. Anything is enough if it be pure; but purity itself comes to things from the simplicity of the spirit which regards them, not indeed with indifference, rather with joy, but without any *ulterior* interest; in other words, purity comes of detaching the thing seen and loved from the world that besets and threatens it and attaching it to the spirit to which it is an eternal possession. But this thing eternally possessed by the spirit is not the thing as the world knows and prizes it; it is not the person, or nation, or religion as it asserts and flaunts itself, in a mortal anxiety to be dominant; it is only that thing in its eternal essence, out of which the stress and the doubt of existence have wholly passed. It is that thing dead, immortal, its soul restored, as Plotinus would have said, to the soul of the universe where, together with all other souls, it has always been contained in its purity and perfection. But the truth of it *there* is not the fact of it *here*; and therefore the world, though the spirit loves it far more truly and tenderly than it loves itself, is chilled and rebuked by that look of divine love, which, if it were heeded, would transmute its whole life and change it from what it so passionately and cruelly is, in time, into that which the spirit sees it to be in eternity.

XVI

THE human heart is full of political, religious,
metaphysical ambition; it hugs all sorts of
pleasant projects in art and in fortune. These
are moral interests and, if not misguided, may
bring hidden or future facts before the mind,
and broaden the basis for rational action. So
the Platonic philosophy sets the scene in one
way for the play, the Christian system in a way
somewhat different, and modern science, if we
make a naturalistic system out of it, in still
another. I will not say that the question
which of these is true, or truer, is indifferent to
the spirit; its fortunes and temper will evidently vary if it is bred in one or another of
these climates. But if the facts were discovered, whatever they might turn out to be,
the spirit would be equally ready and able to
face them. It is not in the least bound up with
the supposition, whatever it may mean exactly,
that any " values are the most real things in the
universe." What should the spirit care if
moralistic metaphysics ceased to invade the
field of natural philosophy, venturing there
upon some guesses flattering to human vanity?
What if the most real—that is, I suppose, the
most fundamental and dynamic—things in the
universe were utterly inhuman? Would spiritu-

ality be thereby prevented from being spiritual, from seeing and judging whatever world happened to exist in the light of spirit?

When I say the *light of spirit* I might as well say *light* simply; for what is spirit but the act of making light actual, of greeting, observing, questioning, and judging anything and everything? Spirit is awareness, intelligence, recollection. It requires no dogmas, as does animal faith or the art of living. Human morality, for the spirit, is but the inevitable and hygienic bias of one race of animals. Spirit itself is not human; it may spring up in any life; it may detach itself from any provincialism; as it exists in all nations and religions, so it may exist in all animals, and who knows in how many undreamt-of beings, and in the midst of what worlds? It might flourish, as the Stoics felt, even in the face of chaos, except that chaos could not sustain the animal life, the psyche, which spirit requires for its organ. From the existence of spirit a psychologist may therefore argue back to the existence—at least local and temporary—of some cosmos of organized matter: but this dependence of mind on body is a lesson taught by natural philosophy, when natural philosophy is sound; it is not a free or evident requirement of spirit in its first deliverance. On the contrary, the body which is the matrix and cradle of spirit in time, seems a stumbling-block to it in its spontaneous

career; and a rather long discipline and much
chastening hardly persuade this supernatural
nursling that it is really so domestic, and that
it borrows its existence from a poor, busy,
precarious animal life; or that the natural
rhythms, pauses, and synthetic reactions of
that life are the ground of its native affinity
with the eternal. Yet such is the fact: spirit,
as I have said, is a hypostatic unity which
makes actual and emotional the merely formal
unities or harmonies of bodily life; and since
the living psyche is in flux, any actual existence which bridged its processes and relations
would have to transcend time in its survey,
and not be attached or confined to any of the
moments which it overlooked and spanned.
Therefore spirit is essentially dateless, and its
immediate terms are essences in themselves
eternal; which is not to say that one form
of spirit does not continually replace another
in the world. There is a continual variation
in themes, and there may be intermittences in
intuition itself; but each of these themes is an
essence overarching a part of the existential
flux, and each moment or node in intuition
looks out of its narrow window upon a vista
which, whether broad or confined, is not
anchored in the place of any of its sundry
objects.

To this organ and to this temporal basis
spirit can accommodate itself perfectly when

once it has discovered them. Naturalism has its modest way of doing the spirit honour. In whatever manner natural forces may operate, if ever they issue in life, it can be only because they already have established rhythms, such as day and night, favourable to that life, to its renewal and inheritance. Any world, any society, any language has a natural inertia or tendency to continue; it satisfies and encourages the spirit which it creates. It fits the imagination because it has kindled and moulded it, and it satisfies its resident passions because these are such, and such only, as could take root and become habitual in precisely that world. This natural harmony between the spirit and its conditions is the only actual one: it is the source of every ideal and the sole justification of any hope. Imperfect and shifting as this harmony must be, it is sufficient to support the spirit of man; and if this spirit be clear and open, it is sufficient to unroll before it all the proper objects of its contemplation in their invincible beauty and eternity. That the vision, considered as an event in history, must change and pass is indifferent. It is not because other people love what I love that, if I am a free spirit, I love it, nor because I have always loved it or must always love it in future, but because it is lovely as I see it now. Such is the assurance that is proper to life, to actuality, to intuition: the rest is weariness of spirit, and a burden to the flesh. But the animal in man is wretched unless he can imagine that his language, nation, arts, and sentiments are destined to be supreme in the world for ever; he is hardly content to suppose that he may not rise again to take part in celebrating some final, yet unending, victory; and he demands eternity not for the lovely essences which he may have beheld, which have eternity in themselves already, but for the manifestation of those essences, which cannot have it.

XVII

Since spirit is an emanation of natural life
there would be impiety on its part in flouting
or denying its own source: yet this has always
been a temptation for spirit when self-conscious
and self-contained: hence the pride of Lucifer,
the mock independence of the Stoic sage, the
acosmism and absoluteness of the Indian
mystic, and the egotism of German philosophy,
thinking to create and recreate its world in
its flight through nothingness. The trouble
with such forced attitudes is that they attempt
to divorce spirituality from piety, which is the
other half, and the fundamental half, of a
sound religion. In Platonism and Christianity
this divorce has been avoided, but without
establishing a happy and stable marriage;
because the object of piety is the power, whatever it may be, on which life depends; and it
is not true piety to invent or posit other sources
for life or welfare than those which experience
shows to exist: piety is wisdom. Nor does the
spiritual life profit in the end by trespassing in
this way on the preserves of a sober piety and a
sober science; because the spirit is thereby
entangled in the fanatical defence of fantastic
dogmas, as if these were indispensable to its
life; so that its peace is poisoned, and its

wings are clipped. What folly to suppose that ecstasy could be abolished by recognizing the true sources of ecstasy! Yet ecstatic, and not addressed to matters of fact, the spirit is in its essence, whenever it arises at all. It actualizes, in an intuition which is through and through poetical and visionary, various movements, rhythms, potentialities, and transcendent relations which physical life involves but which are not parts or moments of its moving substance, and remain merely formal facts for the external observer.

The attachment of spiritual minds to some particular system of cosmology, Platonic, Christian, Indian, or other, is, therefore, a historical accident—a more or less happy means of expression, but a treacherous article of faith. The truth of any of these systems is a question for science, not at all a postulate of the spiritual life. Accordingly, as Dean Inge says, " an entirely open mind towards the discoveries of science " would be characteristic of a purely spiritual religion. But it is not possibly characteristic of a convinced Platonist or a convinced Christian. In Platonism, as in Christianity, the spiritual life is not pure, but incarnate in a particular body of dogma, historical and cosmological: both systems are pledged to the magic ascendancy of certain supernatural powers, posited in order to guarantee certain particular human values. No such system, giving an unnatural fixity, in a special cosmos, to a special morality or civilization or to a private personality, can look upon the hypotheses of a free science with anything but terror, perhaps mitigated by contempt: terror, because it has laid up its treasure in an eventual material heaven, which it feels in its bones to be mythical; and perhaps contempt, because free science is but human discourse, in which one shaky hypothesis is always replacing another; whereas the dogmas of an allegorical religion, for the very reason that they express elementary human feelings and fancies, can appeal to the heart so long as the heart is human. To cultivate this contempt for free science, and to endure that terror with fortitude, aided by hypnotic ritual influences and the contagion of many voices crying in unison, must be the policy of any such system; it must stand by its guns. It can cultivate its own learning and arts and philosophy, but with free science it can have nothing to do. It is not to-day or yesterday, as Dean Inge seems to think, that science has discredited these mythical dogmas. Science is but a name for consecutive observation and understanding, and science had amply disproved those dogmas before they arose: a fact which did not prevent them from arising and from prevailing exceedingly.

The interests which these dogmas expressed

and sanctioned were respectable interests,
political, moral, and emotional. The civilized
mind is still very much more at home in such
a cosy world than in the universal flux of
nature, which not only opens material im-
measurable abysses on every side of our human
nest, but threatens us with an indefinite flux in
our own being, in our habits, institutions,
affections, and in the very grammar and cate-
gories of our thought. Yet neither science nor
spirituality share this classic dislike or fear of
the infinite. Science, although its occasion is
the description and manipulation of the field
of action, is heartily willing to describe it and
manipulate it in any convenient way. It is
perhaps the best sign of a scientific, as distinguished from a doctrinaire, temper not to
lay great store on science itself, that is, on its
forms, language, and theories, but to keep it
plastic in the presence of its existing subject-
matter, and of the spontaneity of human
fancy, which, at any moment, may suggest new
methods of notation, new abbreviations, new
syntheses. As to spirit, it has a far deeper
reason than science for eluding every conven-
tion and not regarding institutions, whether
political, ecclesiastical, or intellectual, with
more than a resigned courtesy. Such things
must needs be: it would be foolish to reject
them instead of profiting by them. The body,
which is an institution of nature, is the indis-

pensable organ of spirit in man; political and religious institutions are organs necessary also for certain kinds of spiritual life; and if the cosmos, too, is a permanent institution, the spirit can very well acknowledge that accidental fact and submit, *here*, to the limitations thereby imposed upon it. But it would be, for spirit, a limitation; its proper field is *there*, in the world which is eternal by inward necessity and essence, not by a longevity presumed to be perpetual; a world which for the same reason is infinite, as a world of change, even if endless, cannot be, since it expressly excludes any order of events other than the one which it happens to realize.

XVIII

THE Platonists, like all typical Greeks, shuddered at the infinite and hardly thought of it, even in the optical form of infinite space. This is of itself a sufficient proof that they were fundamentally political philosophers, moralists, humanists, and not men living primarily in the spirit. They thought the infinite formless—a conception which is possible only in the absence of concentration upon that idea; for, when considered intently, the infinite is seen to contain all forms: it is the realm of essence. This observation, if they had stopped to make it (and it requires no special intelligence, only pause) would have dispelled any aesthetic dislike which they may have had of the infinite; yet it would not have changed their radical indifference to it. The Greeks were not aesthetes; their love of form and their approach to perfection in it were not aesthetic but moral, political, hygienic: like noble animals they were proud and content in their own bodies, faculties, and loves; words could not express their indifference to what was not human; and when some divine shaft rent those bodies and blackened that mind, the cry of their mourning was brief but absolute. Their love of finitude was vital; it was the love of existence, and of perfection in existence; and for that reason, not for any idle aestheticism, they were clear discerners of beauty. Aestheticism is incapable of producing the beautiful or, in the end, even of loving or discerning it; it has cut off the vital and moral roots of form which render one form more beautiful than another, and which, deeper still, give unity of form to objects at all. These vital roots of form were alive in the Greeks: they flowered into sundry finite perfections; and evidently they could not flower into forms contrary to these particular perfections, rooted in a particular living seed, limited to the play of a particular animal body and its appropriate mind. The infinite was valueless: and from the moral point of view, from the point of view of some natural organism striving to be free and perfect, valueless the infinite certainly is.

But spirit is a terribly treacherous inmate of the animal soul; it has slipped in, as Aristotle says, from beyond the gates: and its home is the desert. This foreignness is moral, not genealogical: spirit is bred in the psyche because the psyche, in living, is obliged to adjust herself to alien things: she does so in her own interest: but in taking cognizance of other things, in moulding a part of her dream to follow their alien fortunes, she becomes intelligent, she creates spirit; and this spirit overleaps the pragmatic function of physical

sensibility—it is the very act of overleaping it
—and so proves itself a rank outsider, a child
rebellious to the household, an Ishmael ranging
alone, a dweller in the infinite.

This infinite is the infinite of forms, the
indestructible and inevitable infinite that contains everything, but contains it only in its
essence, in that eternal quality of being in
which everything is a companion and supple-
ment to everything else, never a rival or a contradiction. These essences, when thought considers any of them without knowing whether
they describe any earthly object or not, may
be called ideal; but they are not ideal intrinsically, either in the sense of being figments of
thought or of being objects of aspiration. They
become ideal, or enter into an external moral
relation to the animal soul, when this soul
happens to conceive them, or to make them
types for the objects of its desires. A perfectly
free spirit (if it could exist) would not consider
eternal beings in their ideal capacity, because
it would no longer refer them to the fancies or
hopes of some living creature, but would consider them in themselves, ranging from one to
another quite speculatively, that is, guided by
the intrinsic formal relations of similarity or
inclusion which obtain between them. It
would therefore virtually traverse the infinite,
its path not being hedged in by pre-existing
irrelevant interests in one form of being rather

than in another. But evidently this perfect impartiality is not human; it is contrary to the initial status of spirit, as the hypostatic synthetic expression and realization of some discursive phase of animal life—some adventure, some predicament, some propensity, some preoccupation. It is therefore natural that the intrinsic infinity of Being should remain in the background, even in the spiritual life, and that essences should be contemplated and distinguished rather as ideals for the human imagination than as beings necessary in themselves.

XIX

FOR this reason the Platonic philosophy opens a more urbane and alluring avenue towards spiritual enlightenment than does the Indian, although the latter runs faster towards the goal and attains it more perfectly. The limitation of the divine intellect, or the Ideas, to the types of earthly or celestial bodies, and to the values proper to their lives, leaves the afterglow of passion upon them; the eternal profits by the interest which its worshippers have in the temporal. This accommodation is also conspicuous in the Catholic tradition: it seems doubtful sometimes whether that other world is a liberation from this one, or a re-duplication of it, with all its temporal, moral, social, and diplomatic business extended indefinitely. This is the price which the spiritual life has to pay for being made amiable. A universe is composed on purpose to facilitate it; life there becomes so easy and natural, it retains so many human values, that it threatens to be choked in a system of anxious hopes and adjustments, worse than those involved in mundane life, because inescapable. In this world, at least, the spirit can flee to solitude, to nature, to play, to the delicious irony of despising the passions which one is forced to

share; but from heaven, ennobled and sancti-
fied as it would be by so many immortal per-
sonages, so many high maxims, marvellous
dogmas, and moral exclusions, whither should
the spirit flee? Of course the spiritual sense
for those celestial facts might be recovered;
even in heaven one might be a philosopher.
The other world would be but a second touch-
stone for the spirit if, like this world and its
moral order, it were a fact existing in itself.
In the Catholic, as in the Platonic, kingdom,
the spirit must still blaze its own trail; the
carpets spread accommodatingly before its
feet, leading to the celestial courts, will never
lead it, of themselves, to spiritual liberation.

Consider the universe of Plotinus: a process
of emanation from the One through the Ideas
to the Soul of the World, whence, like rays
from different stars, human and animal souls
descend on occasion to animate material
bodies. This system was designed to encourage
the spirit to rise from its animal prison—
prison was the word—reversing that emanation
until it recovered the primal bliss of contemplative union with pure Being. But what is
there in the system, if we accept it as describing
the facts, to compel or even to invite the spirit
to rise at all? The cosmology of Plotinus
might almost be adopted by a Hegelian inter-
ested only in evolution and not in the least in
redemption; he might behold with rapture the

successive embodiment of linked Ideas in the
thoughts and institutions of men; far from
wishing to reverse the process in his heart, and
renounce all these endless transformations,
conflicts, and cumulative cares, his only joy
might be to share them, to be the first to
announce them, and at every turn in the battle
to drop the cry of yesterday in order to pick
up that of to-morrow. Since it was the nature
of things to emanate from the One, he would
hasten to emanate with them. All his angels
would be seen descending Jacob's ladder, and
none ascending. Yet only the ascent concerns
the spiritual life. The descent is the creation
of the world and the work of the world, by
which the spirit, when it awakes at last, finds
itself entangled in animal passions and foolish
ambitions. Starting from whatever facts and
predicaments may seem to envelop it, its
function is then to detach itself from them one
by one, escaping the flux and urgency which
they have in the realm of existence, unravelling
and synthesizing their temporal perspectives,
in order to transpose them all into the realm
of truth, where they form an eternal picture;
and then to let this picture itself recede into its
setting in the realm of essence, where it is but
one form of being, which this world by chance
has manifested, amid the countless forms of
being which perhaps have not been manifested
anywhere. The angels, even in their descent,

will then be messengers to the philosopher from an eternal world, to which, in ascending again, they carry up his heart; whereas if the angels were born in transit and lived only in their apparition in time, he might have perhaps a pleasanter casual environment, but no heavenly treasure; and his attitude would be that of a lover and gloating denizen of this world, not that of the spirit. Even from the best world the spirit must depart. Beauty calls it away no less than confusion; and happiness is only a more amiable sacrament than suffering to carry it to the impassible Being which infinitely outruns all these accidents of exist-ence.

XX

Spirit, since its essence is to aspire, comes to life at the foot of the ladder; it lives by contemplation, by knowing the thing above it. It is not its own object, as the Platonic Ideas seemed to become in Aristotle's theology, when they were identified with a cosmic intellect eternally contemplating its own structure. Spirit might indeed attain to such a condition if its natural organ were, as Aristotle supposed, some perfectly harmonious and immortal revolution of the heavens. Even then spirit would properly be the rapt aspiration towards those Ideas, the immortal love of them, which kept the moving spheres constant in their round: for the soul of each sphere was intently fixed upon the Idea (or, as we might say, the formula) which it was to realize by its motion and to turn into a sustained note in the celestial symphony. Even in this astronomical theology spirit would be the third person of the Trinity rather than the second; it would be the Soul of the World looking towards the Ideas, rather than the Ideas looking towards the One. This One, if we may identify it with the Brahma of the Indians, would be infinite Being; it would not be any longer conformable or proper to any particular cosmos or to any particular moral life. Relevance to nature would begin with the divine intellect or the sphere of the Platonic Ideas: they would be finite in number and exclusive in type; they would compose the morphology of this world. The third person or hypostasis in the eternal, would be the divine spirit, the love or attention by which those particular forms were made the theme of an actual life. This divine spirit looks towards the Ideas; it is hardly different from the God of Aristotle; and it may be said to descend (although inwardly still wholly attentive to the beings above it) and to animate the world, in the sense in which heavenly souls may be said to descend to animate our bodies; namely, in that an echo or imitation of them or obedience to them keeps the world or the body alive. The immortal soul of the world could never itself look downwards or be troubled by the vicissitudes of the matter which imitates its form: no more could the immortal soul of any man be compromised by the imperfections of its earthly shadow.

We are here in the region of speculative fiction; souls have become so perfect in their eternal abode that other souls have to take their places in living bodies. Indeed, an organic inherited soul, a principle of material growth and action, is no spirit; spirit is first generated in it when it awakes to some actual feeling or thought. Such a spirit evidently can never envisage pure Being, or the realm of essence, in its infinite fullness and detail; the essences which will appear to it will be such, and such only, as its material organ evokes by its quite special processes and contacts. But quantity is not a category important to spirit; as it is indifferent to duration, because it lives in the eternal, so it is indifferent to the endless multiplicity of things, existing or not existing, which may lie beyond its ken. It is not anxious, like an animal soul hounded by curiosity and fear, to dominate and possess everything, lest by overlooking some secret enemy it should live in a fool's paradise, and to-morrow be ruined. The limitations of experience, when experience is spiritual, are not invidious; what it possesses it cannot lose; what it leaves out is not denied or condemned or demanded. As Dante says, there is no envy in these spheres. The sense that the rest is there (since all essences are implied in infinite Being) suffices to give the spirit room, to detach it from all partiality, from all unjust affection; while the essential eternity of that which is manifested suffices to wed the spirit to it with an absolute confidence, without the least ignoble hankering to look beyond. Spirit differs from animal intelligence less in material scope than in inward quality; its distinctive object is not pure Being in its infinity, but finite being in its purity.

XXI

EVEN in rare moments of attainment, when the human spirit has seemed to be united or even identified with the supreme Being, the reports which reach us of that ecstasy indicate that the chasm has never really been bridged. These reports are avowedly inadequate; words cannot render what has been seen, nor would it be lawful, perhaps, to reveal it. Ultimate insights have a tendency to undermine the orthodox approaches by which they have been reached. The saint pulls his ladder up with him into his private heaven; and the community of the faithful, on whose sturdy dogmatic shoulders he has climbed, must not be deprived of the means of following his example. Hence any dissolving culmination of the religious life must be kept a secret, a mystery to be divulged only to the few whom the knowledge of it can no longer scandalize or discourage. Besides this prudence and this consideration for the weaker brethren, there is a decisive reason for silence: the revelation has been essentially a revelation of the illusion inherent in all language, in all experience, in all existence. It cannot be communicated save by being repeated.

Doubtless the state of being achieved in ecstasy is intrinsically immensely positive, but

it is the negation of every human wish and idea;
there are, and can be, no human words to
express its nature. So true is this, that if the
mystic uses this very suspension of thought, this
ecstasy itself, as a true rendering of his ultimate
object of contemplation, he falls into a worse
error than the animal and worldly mind. For
at least, in current experience, scattered and
accidental manifestations of being appear;
they are illusions if taken for more than appear-
ances, relative to particular animal organs and
interests; they are trivial and competitive;
yet they are distinct, and each of them, by its
positive character, enriches that revelation of
essence to spirit which animal life necessarily
affords, in spite of its distraction. It would
suffice to suspend the urgency of the animal
will (as sometimes happens to children and
poets in their simplicity) in order to disinfect
this sensuous revelation of its distraction and
illusion; it would not reveal much, but it
would reveal something of pure Being. In
poets and children this is but play; they revert
from it at once to what the world thinks serious
interests and sound knowledge of facts. When
on the contrary the same disillusion is attained
laboriously, by a long spiritual discipline, the
adept attempts to maintain and propagate his
insight; and then there is trouble, for in the
very act of defending this insight, he is likely
to lose it. In so far as the objects of his con-

templation are familiar to everyone and have
accepted names, these names will carry animal
faith with them, and when he uses them they
will conceal or even contradict the new quality
of pure being which things have acquired in his
eyes; to him they have become eternal
essences, to his hearers they will still be
temporal facts. Meantime, in that realm of
essence which he now envisages, vistas may
have opened to him into all sorts of regions
which are not of this world, which have no
names at all in human discourse; how should
he be able to express or even to remember their
intricate and unearthly nature? Even in
ordinary dreams, composed as they are,
presumably, out of bits of earthly imagery and
puffs of animal anxiety, there are many
marvels and vicissitudes, momentous to themselves, which we cannot recover in the light
of day: how much harder the vision must be
to recompose if its elements were original or its
mood sublime! If spiritual attainment could
ever be complete and infinite Being could
reveal itself (which I do not believe) in its
entirety, evidently the disproportion would be
overwhelming between the number and variety
of things to report and the human means of
reporting them.

Silence is therefore imperative, if the mystic
has any conscience; he cannot have perceived,
and he cannot retain, the fullness of his ultimate

object. This fullness came to him, and remains in him, merely as a *sense* of fullness, the brilliancy of a blinding light, without any specification of the infinity of essences which were there to be lighted up. He therefore can only assure us that it was a great revelation, freeing him from the oppression of ordinary existence and thought; it was peace, it was bliss, it was virtual knowledge; but beyond that his powers of perception and retention could not go.

XXII

HERE the mystic—he who feels he has passed beyond the veil and seen things not to be uttered—if he lacks humility and discipline, may fall, and may lead us, into a sad illusion. He may take his dazzled feeling itself, the blinding glory of mere light, for the supreme reality, or for the true description of its nature. He may say that infinite Being is itself simply feeling, or intensity without quality or distinctions, or the pure light of spirit falling, not on everything, but only on itself. He would then be confusing his own incapacity with the object which infinitely exceeds it. The glass dome, far from creating the many colours of infinite Being, fuses and neutralizes them into a white light—the blurred effect of a rude and summary vision. This unitary feeling, rather than a revelation of pure Being, is the customary sense of one's own bodily existence. The words existence and being are often used interchangeably, and this verbal ambiguity serves to obscure the infinite difference between the realm of essence—pure Being in all its eternal modes—and the pressure of external things and of internal change in a living organism. This sense of existence, essentially transitive and restless, may sometimes be lulled into a

simmering warmth and voluminous comfort, a
pleasant animal trance in which spirit dives as
deep as it can into the life of the matter. This
feeling has a true depth of its own, a kinship
with universal substance. Brahma is sometimes likened to deep sleep, and Nirvana to
nothingness; and in modern philosophy we are
sometimes told that the true reality is pure
duration or pure sentience. These expressions
ignore pure Being, and even the presumable
substance of the natural world, which must
somehow be diversified and unevenly distri-
buted; but they describe fairly enough the
sentiment which the presence of overwhelming
things inspires, or the trail which their passage
leaves in the animal mind. Persons far
advanced in the spiritual life often use language
of this kind, as they use pious or erotic language; but their language must not be taken
amiss; they use, like all of us, the words they
find. To the true mystic even things are
symbols; how should he worship words? The
Spanish mystic, for instance, San Juan de la
Cruz, represents all virtues and graces as by-
paths diverging from the straight but difficult way, the name of which is Nothing,
Nothing, Nothing. In the end the spirit
indeed claims nothing, posits nothing, and is
nothing in its own eyes, but empties itself
completely into the Being which it contem-
plates; but if this Being itself were said to be

G

nothing, our mysticism would evidently have slipped into a bad heresy, not to speak of the flat contradiction. So Nirvana may be called annihilation in that it annihilates personality, desire, and temporal existence; yet the "Buddha teaches that all beings are from eternity abiding in Nirvana"[1] so that far from being nothing Nirvana embraces the whole realm of essence—pure Being in its infinite implications—from which, of course, existence is excluded; because since existence is necessarily in flux and is centred in some arbitrary moment, it itself exists only by exclusion and with one foot in the grave. Existence is that realm of Becoming which combines Being and Non-Being so much to Hegel's satisfaction, and which generates those unstable but " current valuations of the worldling " to which the spirit, according to Dean Inge, is so completely indifferent.

[1] Dasgupta, *History of Indian Philosophy*.

XXIII

THE spiritual life, then, is distinguished from
worldly morality and intelligence not so much
by knowledge as by disillusion: however
humble may be its career, it lifts those few and
common adventures into the light of eternity.
This eternal aspect of things summons spirit
out of its initial immersion in sensation and in
animal faith and clarifies it into pure spirit.
This eternal aspect of things is also their immediate aspect, the dimension in which they are
not things but pure essences; for if belief and
anxiety be banished from the experience of
any object, only its pure essence remains
present to the mind. And this aspect of
things, which is immediate psychologically,
ontologically is ultimate, since evidently the
existence of anything is a temporary accident,
while its essence is an indelible variation of
necessary Being, an eternal form. The spirit
lives in this continual sense of the ultimate in
the immediate. Mortal spirits, the spirit in
animals, cannot possibly survey pure Being in
its infinity; but in so far as they free themselves from false respect for the objects of
animal faith and animal passion, they may
behold some finite being in its purity. For this
reason, established morality and religion, by

protecting the eye from too much distraction
and fixing it on noble objects, may make a
better soil for spirit than does wayward living.
Not that spirit may not crop out marvellously
in the sinner, as it may in the child or the poet.
It notoriously does so; and even in the saint
it remains profoundly indifferent to the occasion that may have kindled its flame, be this
occasion religious faith or sensuous vision, be it
passion, study, or practical dominion over the
world. All is grist for the mill, if only there
be force of intellect actually to grind that
experimental substance and reduce it to some
pure essence on which contemplation can feed.
But moralities and religions, if they merely
extend or exaggerate the pressure of circum-
stance on the soul, are as dreadful an incubus
on the spirit as ever was the animal search for
food, love, or safety; indeed, they are but a
monstrous and terrifying shadow of these
radical compulsions cast needlessly on the
screen of heaven.

I ask myself sometimes, is not morality a
worse enemy of spirit than immorality? Is it
not more hopelessly deceptive and entangling?
Those romantic poets, for instance, whose lives
were often so irregular—were they not evidently
far more spiritual than the good people whom
they shocked? Shelley, Leopardi, Alfred de
Musset were essentially children of the spirit:
they were condemned to flutter on broken

wings only for lack of measure and discipline; they were spiritual waifs, untaught to see the relativity and absurdity of their proud passions. The perfect spirit must be a patient hearer, a sober pupil, not an occasional automatic sky-lark. Yet when spirituality, as in Words-worth, has to struggle instead against a black coat and a white choker, it seems to be more sadly and decisively stifled, buried alive under a mountain of human alarms and a heavy tombstone of sanctimony. The world, he sighed, is too much with us; but the hills and even the mock Tritons blowing their wreathed horns were not able to banish the world from his conscientious concern. Nothing is able to banish the world except contempt for the world, and this was not in him. It would even have been contrary to his Protestant religion —that so unspiritual determination to wash the world white and clean, adopt it, and set it up for a respectable person. The world is not respectable; it is mortal, tormented, confused, deluded for ever; but it is shot through with beauty, with love, with glints of courage and laughter; and in these the spirit blooms timidly, and struggles to the light among the thorns.

Such is the flitting life of this winged thing, spirit, in this old, sordid, maternal earth. On the one hand, in its innocence, spirit is happy to live in the moment, taking no thought for the morrow; it can enjoy the least gift as gladly as the greatest; it is the fresh, the pure voice of nature, incapable of learned or moral snobbery. It ignores its origin, so buoyant is it; its miraculous light seems to it a matter of course. Its career is everywhere conditioned and oppressed from without, yet it passes through the fire with a serene incredulity, an indomitable independence. On the other hand, the eye of spirit, in its virtual omniscience, sees the visible in its true setting of the invisible; it is fixed instinctively on the countless moments that are not this moment, on the joys that are not this sorrow and the sorrows that are not this joy, on the thousand opinions that are not this opinion and beauties that are not this beauty; understanding too much to be ever imprisoned, loving too much ever to be in love. Spirit chills the flesh and is itself on fire; thought, as Dean Inge says, " becomes passionate, the passions become cold "; or rather they are confronted and controlled by a profound recollection, in which laughter and tears pulse together like the stars in a polar sky, each indelibly bright, and all infinitely distant.

XXIV

If with these considerations in mind I turn
back to the characteristics of Dean Inge's
" Platonic tradition in religious thought " I find
that some of these characteristics belong to the
spiritual life everywhere, but not to the
Platonic system. Such is openness to science,
or (what this openness implies) tolerance of any
dogmatic conception, and readiness to accept
any kind of world. Other characteristics are
indeed proper to Platonism, but irrelevant to
the spiritual life; such is the mythical cosmology meant to secure the perpetual preval-
ence of particular human or divine goods, in a
particular Hellenic universe. Still other characteristics seem to belong both to the spiritual
life and to Platonism; but I find on closer
inspection that these qualities are ambiguous,
and are not assignable to both in the same
sense. Of these apparently common properties
the most important is the gift of seeing the
eternal in the temporal. But what is the
eternal? For pure spirit the eternal means the
timeless; all images of sense and all events in
time offer eternal themes for contemplation
and are themselves eternal in the realm of truth.
This spiritual insight has been frequent among
Platonists, and may indeed have been at the

root of that trance-like vision of essences
which enabled Plato to turn the general terms
of Socratic logic into individual and immortal
beings. But, if his sense for the eternal had
been absolutely direct and pure, he would have
seen the eternal in the figments of sense, no less
than in those of logic or ethics: for all forms
equally are essences, and all essences equally
are eternal.

It is true that " things seen are temporal,"
if by " seeing " we understand that animal
reaction by which we turn towards material
objects which affect our eyes, so that we are
prompted to grasp them or to get out of their
way. This animal sensibility is what has
usually been understood by sense, so that sense
has been conventionally regarded as revealing
matter, and a man immersed in sense as a
materialist. But this kind of " seeing," if it
be more than a bodily reaction, is also more
than a pure intuition: it is a belief. Sense
thereby engages the spirit in the observation
and pursuit of material things; and these
obviously are temporal. But in this belief and
pursuit pure intuition must have intervened
to supply the terms of the experience; and
this pure intuition is no vision of material
things, but of the essences which we call and
think to be the qualities of material things, or
of whatever else we think about; and these
essences in themselves are eternal forms of

Being. One whose attention was wholly absorbed in them would be an extreme idealist, a poet or dreamer not suspecting that he was living in a material world, falling into every pit, and hugging every ghost to his bosom, as the most solid of possible realities. And though the world would laugh at him, the angels would not; for after life is done, and the world is gone up in smoke, what realities may the spirit of a man boast to have embraced without illusion, save the very forms of those illusions by which he has been deceived? These, and not the things which he thought he saw, were his eternal discoveries.

In the Platonic system, however, the eternal also has another signification; it may mean the everlasting. This system was cosmological and quasi-scientific; it sought for the substances and the permanent shapes of existing things. God, the Ideas, and the Soul of the World, though invisible, were in a wide sense physical, since they were powers at work in nature. Like the laws of modern physics they were presumed to be unchangeable; but this persistence of their expression in matter was evidently an entirely different sort of eternity—a presumptive eternity—from that intrinsic to them as essences. Yet the same word *eternal* designates now the pure objects of the contemplative faculty and now certain special objects of scientific presumption, belief in which is unnecessary, audacious, and, to be frank, superstitious. That anything existent should be eternal in the spiritual sense is logically impossible, because existence has to verify itself from moment to moment and must always remain temporal, no matter how long it lasts. That any recognizable existing thing should last for ever seems improbable and contrary to all the analogies of nature. It is contrary, too, to that profound natural philosophy of Heraclitus which Plato had adopted and which, by a happy counterblast, had quickened his sense for the truly eternal—for the inviolate and super-existential being of forms.

If this hazardous belief in permanent natural powers were abandoned the comfortable moral assurances of Platonism would also lapse. It would cease to be popular with tender minds, and a nest of sentimental fancies. The beauty and goodness actually found in the world would no longer be alleged to reveal the forces at work in it more truly than do its ugliness and confusion. It would become impossible to maintain that goodness and beauty are somehow intentional in the world, and their opposites interlopers. Values would be seen not to be powers, but harmonies—the very thing which Plato, in his purely moral wisdom, had made the first and highest principle of the good. Indeed, that superstitious belief, with which he thought to buttress the crumbling virtues of antiquity, is useless to human morals. Human morals draw their vigour from earthly economy, and find their sanction there. Nor is that superstitious belief helpful to the spiritual life or even compatible with it at bottom. For while to accept and love the constituted order of nature and society is easy for a pure spirit, which is without prejudices or claims, for this same reason it is impossible for spirit to deny or detest the other forms of being which nature or society for the moment does not happen to manifest.

XXV

The manner of combining unworldliness with the love of nature and of man is another point not understood in the same sense in Platonism and in the spiritual life. Platonism is moralistic: it will love in man and in nature so much as conforms to the patterns which its mathematical physics, its zoology, and its political idealism prescribe for things: all that deviates from these norms will seem to it sad, unaccountable, terrible, and dangerous. In fact, the love of nature and of man, though the beauty of order and harmony in both was still felt in the Greek manner, does not seem to me conspicuous in Platonism. It was a censorious, puritan, prescriptive love; it was not spontaneous, it was not sympathetic, it was not love of nature at all, but of a political, human good, and of so much in nature as might illustrate or sanction it. Free spirit would be more generous. When the renunciation of the world, and of existence itself, has been hearty and radical, the love of nature can be universal; I will not say unqualified by sadness, because the spirit, having itself suffered, recognizes in many an alien form of existence a maimed effort and a lost glory analogous to its own; but a love unqualified by prejudice, by envy, by fear of being outshone or discountenanced by the marvels which nature or society may elsewhere bring to light. It is of the essence of spirit to see and love things for their own sake, in their own nature, not for the sake of one another, nor for its own sake.

Meantime it is a question for scientific speculation, on which pure spirit remains ignorant and impartial, whether there are in existence organisms so vast (measured by the human scale) as the Platonic cosmos, with its deity or deities animating its concentric spheres. If so, spirit would have for its habitation and organ other bodies larger and more long-lived than the bodies of men or of kindred animals: and the concert of so many happier spirits would certainly be sublime, singing in their Pythagorean symphony so calmly together. Yet even then, we should remember that the human scale is relative, and that this Platonic cosmos (or the Christian cosmos which, though historical rather than astronomical, is not very different in principle) is vast only in that perspective. Seen from without, and beyond, it might be infinitesimal, and an insignificant ingredient in some greater world. Its longevity, too, would be relative; and the traditional attribution of eternity to it must be regarded as a rhetorical hyperbole, expressing the sense that its duration is incalculable in terms of human chronology; but true eternity, as I have said, is not of that kind. In the end such a universe, floating like a bubble in the flux of things, would almost certainly dissolve. It is not there that an enlightened heart would lay up its treasure. The flood itself is a nobler companion, and the spirit moves at ease upon the waters.

OPINION OF THE WORK OF
GEORGE SANTAYANA

A LIST OF SANTAYANA'S BOOKS MAY BE HAD FROM ANY BOOKSELLER

LONDON: CHARLES WHITTINGHAM AND GRIGGS (PRINTERS), LTD.
CHISWICK PRESS, TOOKS COURT, CHANCERY LANE.